A Portrait
of
BILLY GRAHAM

presented by

ASHEVILLE
CITIZEN-TIMES
VOICE OF THE MOUNTAINS • CITIZEN-TIMES.com

The Courier-Journal
(LOUISVILLE, KY)

THE TENNESSEAN
Every day matters.   www.tennessean.com

The Greenville News

ACKNOWLEDGEMENTS

The *Asheville Citizen-Times* wishes to thank Bob Terrell for his commitment to this publication. Without Bob's insight and the experiences he personally shared with the Reverend Billy Graham, this book would not have been possible. The staff at the *Asheville Citizen-Times* that was fortunate enough to work on this project never realized what a wonderful experience they would all share. Bob Terrell offered many stories, some funny, others sad, but certainly all were insightful into the wonderful man Billy Graham is. In some ways this project has made us all feel a little closer to someone we thought was larger than life. We commend the Reverend Billy Graham for all the lives he has touched, including ours.

We also must thank those that have been a part of our archived history at the *Asheville Citizen-Times,* the Billy Graham Evangelistic Association and photographer Russ Busby. Without their preservation of our past, the clippings and photos you see throughout the book would not have been possible. History once told is an incredible journey, history lost can never be shared. We hope you enjoy your journey.

Bob Terrell

Asheville Citizen-Times

President & Publisher . . . . .Virgil L. Smith

Advertising Director . . . . .Pamela J. Browning

Custom Publishing Manager . . . . .Debbie Wiersma

Custom Publishing Editor . . . . .Jennifer Woods

Desktop Publisher . . . . .Tami Parcell

Contributing Writer . . . . .Bob Terrell

FOREWORD

This publication celebrates the life of a living legend, the Reverend Billy Graham of Montreat, North Carolina, the world's best-known evangelist.

We present this profile of Reverend Graham, who is captured by unique photographs and stories that have touched the hearts of millions around the world.

We invite you to enjoy this wonderful publication and begin a journey that will impact your life.

Virgil L. Smith
President and Publisher

Virgil L. Smith

This book is dedicated to T. W. Wilson

1919 - 2001

"Ruth and I have lost one of the closest friends we ever had. He was a companion on most of the trips I have taken since 1962 all over the world. We prayed, laughed and wept on hundreds of occasions. I feel his loss very deeply, but I know where he is."

— Billy Graham

Table of Contents

A Portrait Of Billy Graham

BY BOB TERRELL

Somehow the term "electronic evangelist" seemed derogatory, or at least inappropriate, when applied to Billy Graham. While other tel-evangelists fell from grace for committing the same sins they preached against, Billy Graham easily weathered storms that centered around attempts to dig up similar dirt on his ministry.

The preacher from Montreat, North Carolina, deserved more than that. Time and time again through his ministry, Billy stood strong in the face of apparent damning criticism and accusations and survived attacks on his ministry by people who tried to bring it tumbling down. These were notably journalists laboring under the Woodward and Bernstein Syndrome of finding sudden fame by exposing, or attempting to expose, public figures to the scorn of followers and, in Billy's case, the world.

Billy was the most widely known and effective evangelist since the Apostle Paul, thanks again in part to his work on television. It is a fact that his quarterly appearances on television, preaching crusades all over the world, helped establish that identity. The piercing eyes, stabbing finger, and urgent voice exhorting sinners to the cross became known in the far corners of the earth.

He was a man who sat with kings and presidents, who preached to audiences of hundreds of thousands of people — once to more than a million in Korea — a man who brought more people to the foot of the throne than anyone, save Christ himself, in the history of the world. He was a man who was equally at home with the president of the United States or with the lowest peasant in the field.

There are many other facets of Graham's character than that of television evangelist. With fame straddling his shoulders, he had very

Opposite:

Evangelist Billy Graham early in his career.

photo by John Engstead

What It's All About

Someone told Ruth they never dreamed what a crusade was all about. "We thought it was just what we saw on TV," they said, "but learning what a crusade is all about has been an amazing thing. I am beginning to see that the public meetings are just a small part of what it's all about. It is amazing what goes on before and after."

— Billy Graham

little private life all the years he preached, but in that privacy there were other traits about him that stood out, characteristics the public didn't often see — like a great sense of humor — sides that made him the humble, down-to-earth, thoroughly likeable man he is.

If one were to make a chart of Billy Graham and diagram him, a large portion of the diagram would be taken up by compassion. Seldom has the world seen a more compassionate man than Billy, down on his knees in the thick, black mud of India, praying with devastated survivors of a vicious cyclone and tidal wave, and then rebuilding churches destroyed by the murderous wall of water. Or refusing to take down his tent in West Germany because it stood so near the border that people in East Germany could hear him preach. Or tearing down the ropes that segregated his audience at a Chattanooga crusade in 1953.

Such a picture of the noted evangelist could have been painted a hundred times through the years, always with a different brush, with different background, and for different reasons.

Billy Graham's beginnings were normal for a boy growing up on a dairy farm near

Great In Her Own Right

It's very unusual to see a woman of a great man also be great in her own right. They (Ruth and Billy) are both very strong personalities with strong opinions. Often, if you find two great people together, there's competitiveness, but she is so in love with him, I think she'd rather see him get the attention.

She has her own ministry, which includes trips to Michigan's Jackson State Prison to visit inmates. . . . A prisoner convicted of stabbing a man to death said Mrs. Graham had visited him in Jackson State Prison five years ago, and has sent him more than twenty-five letters and classical music tapes.

— Jeanie Ford
Billy Graham's sister

Strength to Lean On

News commentator Paul Harvey said Mrs. Graham has helped her husband handle his fame.

"I used to worry about Billy," said Harvey, who has known Graham for more than thirty years. "When he started out there was all that adulation. I was worried that he might be tilted off balance. But then I met Ruth, and then I relaxed, knowing Billy had that strength on which to lean."

—The Associated Press, 1978

Charlotte, North Carolina, in the 1920s. Born November 7, 1918, four days before the Armistice ended World War I, he was the eldest son of William Franklin Graham and his wife, Morrow Coffey Graham. The family existed by selling milk in Charlotte every day.

Billy longed to be a baseball player, and he was a thoughtful boy, never causing his family too much concern. It seemed inevitable that he should come face to face with God, which happened during a 1934 revival meeting in a wooden tabernacle in Charlotte by a fiery itinerant Kentucky evangelist and prohibitionist named Mordecai Ham. Forever afterward, Billy's waking thoughts were of the strengthening of the Kingdom of God on earth.

Those who knew him in the early years could sense the fire of the Lord within him, burning to get out, and few were surprised when he began accelerating his evangelism in the late 1940s.

The 1949 Los Angeles Crusade boosted him to evangelistic significance, and life was never the same for Graham, who would live in the full glare of national and later international prominence for the rest of his life.

Some say he was turned into an overnight sensation by William Randolph Hearst, publisher of the Hearst chain of American newspapers, who issued an order to his vast chain of papers to "Puff Graham" in that L.A. crusade, but by the time of that crusade, Billy already had both feet on the ground in his ministry, preaching widely in the Youth for Christ movement.

There is no question that Hearst's order escalated Billy's climb to the top, for by the time he left Los Angeles other periodicals had followed Hearst's lead, and Billy was known by the nation.

Billy said he did not know what had prompted Hearst to "kiss" him, to use a journalistic expression. "I think God worked on Mr. Hearst's heart," Billy said. "I never met him or corresponded or conversed with him."

By the time Billy finished that Los Angeles Crusade, America knew he was a special preacher, and his services were in demand across the country. From that point he gradually gained international fame, prompted primarily by two gigantic crusades that captured worldwide attention, the 1954 London crusade that attracted more than two million attendees in three months and the 1957 New York City campaign that ran sixteen weeks and drew almost 2.4 million persons.

A Major Accomplishment

One of the things I accomplished was pulling down the ropes that segregated the crowd in Chattanooga in 1952. Blacks came in large numbers and usually sat with other blacks, but they were free to sit where they wanted. Later that year, Dallas insisted on segregation, and had some arguments. Some clergy pulled out of the crusade. Integration in those days was a giant step. One who insisted took his life in his own hands. We got threats but none were carried out.

— Billy Graham

I Want It Now!

I try to make my sermon subjects current. Once I saw in the Los Angeles Times a full-page ad saying, "I Want It Now!" Buy now, pay later. Our whole generation is saying I Want It Now! I want pleasure now, I want this now, and that now. They don't realize that they've got to pay for it later.

My sermons are on topics of current interest with Biblical applications to our own lives and hearts.

— Billy Graham

From that point on, he was in as much international demand as national.

That his ministry lasted as long as it did, all the while with the trust of the world, is a tribute to the man and his sincerity and faithfulness. He always invited scrutiny and always emerged unscathed.

Billy doubled the time most evangelists spend in the ministry before their stars begin to wane, and he has always said that he had no plans for retirement "until God retires me permanently."

Always a crusader for the downtrodden, Billy faced the ugly realm of segregation of the races and found cause to throw himself into the battle with full force. He studied the Bible cover to cover to find any mention of separation of the races, and, finding none, beat the Supreme Court to the punch for integration. On March 15, 1953, more than a year before the Supreme Court's May 17, 1954 decision ended segregation, Billy opened the first deliberately integrated southern crusade in Chattanooga, Tennessee. Ignoring protests and forecasts of trouble, he made clear to the crusade committee that blacks must be allowed to sit where

they pleased. Arriving at the crusade site and finding sections roped off for black people, he himself tore down the ropes.

To his disappointment, though, black attendance was small and those who came tended to sit together rather than mingle with whites. There were no incidents at the gates or in the seating areas.

Billy never again held a segregated crusade. In some cities — Dallas, for example, in May and June of 1953 — because of the obstinacy of the crusade committee, the stadium was segregated, although not any of the ushers prevented blacks from sitting where they pleased. All subsequent crusades have been integrated.

The press's relationship with Billy, especially the British press's, was frosty at first, but improved as the years went by. Arriving in England for his historic 1954 crusade, he was asked such questions as these by the press: "Who invited you over here, anyway?" "Do you think you can save Britain?" and "What do you plan to do about

Opposite: Billy's love for bright clothes is evident in this photo taken during an interview in the 1970s.

photo by June Glenn Jr.

Below: Press conference in Montreat, December 30, 1975. photo by Malcolm Gamble

Russia?"

The press didn't spare Ruth from its scorn, either. She was quizzed thusly: "Is it true your husband carries around his own special jug of water for baptism?"

During that London crusade, Billy made special efforts to accommodate the press, and at the end of the crusade, things had warmed up between them. As years passed and the press found nothing to write negatively about Billy or his mission, relations softened much more, and today he could even be called popular with the press.

Billy probably did more to influence other evangelists than any other person. In one conference — the ten-day International Conference for Itinerant Evangelists in Amsterdam in 1986

"I'm not going to retire preaching the Gospel till the Lord retires me. If I had a stroke and could not talk, I'd write with my feet or something."

— Billy Graham

— Billy and his staff taught 8,160 evangelists how to go about the Lord's business more effectively. In attendance were representatives of 174 countries and every culture and ethnic group in the world, who are now spreading an expanded Gospel through their own territories. For those who could not afford to attend the conference, the Billy Graham Evangelistic Association paid all expenses.

Billy took evangelization of the world seriously and acted according to Jesus' admonition in Matthew 28:19-20: "Go ye therefore and teach all nations, baptizing them in the name of the Father, and of the Son, and of the Holy Ghost, teaching them to observe all things whatsoever I have commanded you: and, lo, I am with you always, even unto the end of the world."

Billy accepted those words as marching orders and has followed them for more than a half-century, and even though he used the air waves to reach millions with the Gospel, he was much more than an electronic evangelist. The phrase doesn't really begin to describe him.

"The Gospel is the same. Finding new ways to illustrate it is my job."

— Billy Graham

Chapter One

PEOPLE

***L**eft: Second night of the Billy*

Graham Crusade, March 24, 1977.

photo by Gary Fields

***B**elow: Billy sings with Johnny*

Cash and June Carter-Cash at the

Asheville Civic Center, 1977.

photo by Gary Fields

A LASTING PARTNERSHIP

BY BOB TERRELL

Marriages, it is said, are made in heaven. So it is with lasting partnerships, or, at least, with this particular partnership. . . .

The hotel dining room was filled with that early morning aroma of coffee perking and bacon in the pan. Bev Shea was already there. Cliff Barrows came in a minute after we sat down. Both were casually dressed and appeared to be relaxed after a good night's sleep. The interview had been prearranged. I wanted them to talk about the early days with Billy Graham, what the years of their association have meant to them, and particularly how they met and got together.

The atmosphere was conducive to good interviewing. Waitresses moved here and there, and it was warm in the restaurant. Outside, the wind was blustery, and the morning cold. The leaf of a calendar on the wall was turned to March, 1977.

"Ah, gee," Cliff said, running his mind's eye back over thirty years, "what wonderful, wonderful years!"

"Go to the beginning," I urged. "When did you meet Billy?"

Doing God's Work

It probably cost me careerwise, but you don't count the cost when you have a total commitment. I know God gave me every good thing that has come my way because that's what God is. He's good. Good things that he has given me have included some worldly successes so far as my music is concerned, so if God called me to do anything, he called me to be a singer. He has given me some very successful secular record sales. Sometimes he uses things for a beacon to draw people and maybe that's why I've had some of these successes. Hopefully I've got something worthwhile to say now as well as to sing. I still sing all the songs that people request, but at a crusade, I sing the Gospel.

— Johnny Cash, 1977

"We met him in 1945," Cliff said, "my wife, Billie, and I. We had just been married, and we went to Statesville, North Carolina, for a meeting. We wanted to spend a weekend for a honeymoon, so we asked an old gentleman where would be a good place to go. He said, 'Go to the hotel in Lake Lure.'

"We rode a bus to Lake Lure and walked up the long road to the hotel, turning once or twice to admire God's beauty, the lake just across the highway, then the mountains, and above and beyond that the clear blue sky. I felt limitlessly blessed.

"We walked into the hotel and an antiseptic odor filled the lobby. I saw orderlies go by, and I asked what the place was. The man said the navy had taken over the hotel as a rehabilitation center. The war was still going on in the Pacific.

"We were stuck. We had no transportation, no way of getting anywhere. I had a trombone in one hand, a Gladstone suitcase in the other, and Billie carried a couple of cases. At the highway I stuck out my thumb. A fellow stopped in an old car and asked where we were going.

"I said I didn't know and asked if he knew where we could get a room. He said he knew a woman at nearby Chimney Rock who had a couple of rooms over her little store, and he drove us there. The store was beside a small, beautiful stream, filled with large boulders, called the Broad River, although it was only the size of a creek."

"We rented a room," Cliff said. "The woman was a very gracious lady. She let us practice our music on her piano, visited with us, and talked about a man in Asheville named Brown, a man I once knew. He was an old-time musician. We used to call him 'Ninety-Nine Brown' because his favorite song was 'The Ninety and Nine.' He once sang for Billy

Sunday, the baseball player turned evangelist, and for Gypsy Smith, and some others, and he was along in years.

"She telephoned him in Asheville and he invited us to come and spend the night."

On Saturday morning, Ninety-Nine Brown invited them to a youth night service at the Ben Lippen Conference Center. He said a young man named Billy Graham was going to speak.

Although they had never met, Cliff had heard Billy preach once in St. Paul, where Cliff had been an assistant pastor.

Ninety-Nine Brown was a friend of Dr. Robert McQuilkin, founder of the conference

center, and when Brown, Cliff, and Billie were seated, Dr. McQuilkin saw them and came over.

"We've got a little problem, Mr. Brown," he said. "Our song leader had to go home. Would you help us out?"

Brown chuckled, "This is a youth rally, Dr. McQuilkin, and I'm an old man, but I've got a young couple here who I'm sure would be glad to help you." He looked at Cliff and asked, "Wouldn't you?"

"Yes," Cliff said, "we'd love to."

Cliff and Billie were introduced to Billy Graham, who looked at them with a friendly smile, put his arm around Cliff's shoulders, and

Billy's first team (L to R), Ted Smith (pianist), Grady Wilson (associate evangelist), George Beverly Shea (vocalist), Cliff Barrows (music director).

Photo by Jim Edris

Knoxville

Crusade, May 9,

1970. Ruth

Graham, Pat Nixon,

Billy Graham and

Richard Nixon.

photo by June Glenn Jr.

said, "Well, come on, Cliff, we don't have any time to be choosy. Let's go!"

With that, Cliff and Billie took the few steps to the platform, steps that set the course for a lifetime of work.

Looking in retrospect, Cliff said, "Billie and I sang 'It's Real,' and Bill preached on 'Retreat, Overline, and Advance,' I'll never forget that message and I'll never forget that night! Our chance meeting with Bill and Ruth Graham was a providential one."

Four weeks later, Cliff and Billie accompanied evangelist Jack Shuler to Winona Lake. Cliff was Shuler's song leader. He led the singing that evening in the Billy Sunday Tabernacle.

"It was a Youth for Christ function," Cliff said, "and Bill Graham was there. That put us all together again and was the beginning of our relationship. I soon left Jack and started into Youth for Christ work with Bill. We went to England the next year, and we've been together since.

Electronic Problem

At the end of a crusade performance, George Beverly Shea told Cliff Barrows, "Don't call on me again, Cliff; I think I'm losing my voice."

"No, Bev," Cliff replied, "it's not your voice; it's the amplifier."

Someone turned up the amplifier and Bev sounded like himself again.

"At that point," Cliff said, "when we were in Youth for Christ work, I'm sure neither Bill nor I ever dreamed that we would be having meetings like these in England for more than half a century."

Cliff then told of meeting George Beverly Shea, the full-voiced basso-baritone of the Graham team. "I met Bev in 1942," he said. "He doesn't remember me. I was in a college quartet and we were in Chicago. We had sung at the Pacific Garden Mission and then came to Moody Bible Institute for a radio program. Bev was in the control room behind the glass and I thought, Man, he has arrived! If a cat ever looked at a king, that's the way I looked at Bev. I said, 'Ah, man, I'd love to meet him.' "

"I envied *you*," Bev said with twinkles in his eyes.

Cliff laughed. "Yeah, you envied me. We looked like bellhops in our college boy uniforms, and there Bev was. He had arrived. He had already written the great song, 'I'd Rather Have Jesus' ! So I met him, never dreaming that I would have the privilege of working with him the rest of our lives."

"Talk about your association with Billy," I urged.

"It's been my life," Cliff said. "It really has. I like to preach. I like to talk too much. I love to share. In 1948, after we'd been

together a couple of years, there were two or three opportunities to leave the major emphasis of music and preach, either in a church or in Youth for Christ, traveling as one of their evangelists."

Here Cliff paused to explain something. "I always called my Billie, Billie, and called Billy, Bill. I could tell the difference, but I didn't want anybody else getting them mixed up."

On he went with the story then: "Billie and I really prayed about that thing, that the Lord would show us His will, and you know, He spoke to us together so clearly. I remember the

---

They See Billy, When They Can

CHARLOTTE – People insist on seeing Billy Graham and hearing him preach.

Like the young man–possibly just out of his teens–who visited the crusade headquarters in the swank new Wachovia Bank and Trust Co. building.

"I don't suppose it would be possible for me to see Dr. Graham today, would it?" he hesitantly asked. Well, it was Billy's busiest day and he can't possibly see everyone, but. . .

"I don't think so, at all," a local office worker said. "What was it about?"

"Well," said the earnest young man as he clutched his Bible, "I've hitched all the way from New York City. . ."

"Goodness, you could see the President easier," was the rather brusque reply.

Mrs. Mary Folk from Chattanooga, Tenn., couldn't find a ride from the Hotel Barringer out to the Coliseum to hear Billy last Wednesday. It's a good three miles, but Mrs. Folk walked all the way. Only thing was, Mrs. Folk was on crutches and she had to start at 4 p.m. to get a seat for the 7:00 p.m. service. Rides were promptly arranged when the incident came to light.

There's a little, twisted, crippled gnome of a man who sells "The Charlotte News" outside the Selwyn Hotel across the street from crusade headquarters. He is so deformed that he looks literally like a little pile of rags from 25 feet away. but he "sells" Billy Graham. Turned out, when a reporter wondered why, that 20 years ago when Billy was a Charlotte Sunday School teacher, guess who was in his class?

One old man, 70, refused to let Charlotte's crippling bus strike interfere with his hearing Graham preach. He bought a bicycle and rides to and fro every night.

Virginia Booth, a Seattle, Wash., girl who traces a line back to Salvation Army founder William Booth, didn't let transportation worry her, either. One week, unable to get there any other way, she walked every night from Independence Square to the Coliseum where she sang in the choir. that was after working in the crusade office during the day.

GRAHAM JOKES:

A man asked evangelist Billy Sunday on heaven: "Will they chew tobacco in heaven?"

"They might," said Sunday, "but they'll have to go to hell to spit."

Transmigration of souls popped up during a dish washing session one night and hubby asked the little woman who'd subjected him to the sudsy labor: "Honey, does it mean if I die I might come back as a worm?" To which his wife snapped: "No, you never come back as the same thing twice."

Speaking of heavenly bodies, the man said to his pal, "You know, my wife's an angel." To which I answered: "Your lucky, mine's still alive."

ASHEVILLE CITIZEN-TIMES - OCTOBER 19, 1958

Billy chatting

with President

Ronald Reagan and

his wife Nancy at

the White House,

July 19, 1981.

Citizen-Times file photo

day in Philadelphia that we were in the Stratford Hotel—where the Legionnaire's Disease later broke out—that I told Bill, 'You know, after much prayer the Lord's given Billie and me real peace.' Bill didn't know what the future held, but I told him as long as he wanted us to help him that we were committed to the Lord and to him.

"From that day until this I've never had a desire to change my occupation, to go anyplace else. I've never even been tempted. The Lord has handled it. No one ever knows what God's going to do.

"You asked what it has meant to me. It

has been our life, it's been a fulfillment of the purpose of God for our lives, and there's no greater joy than to know that you're in the center of the Will of God, and that this is His will for our lives.

"To my wife," he continued, "who traveled with us the first five years, it meant staying home the next twenty years, spending sixty percent of the time with my being away, just like Bill and Bev. It meant she was going to have to be the daddy as well as the mother, but she had a fixed commitment because we had settled that issue together.

"We found in Bill a man who is not only

sincere and warm but very anxious that his interrelationships with people be as natural and wholesome and filled with concern and integrity as anybody in all the world. I have valued his friendship. It has been genuine, not just a professional thing at crusades and then isolation through the non-crusade days. We've even spent many of our vacations together."

Bev Shea's introduction to Billy Graham was much less complicated than Cliff's.

"I met Billy in 1943," said Bev, he of the golden voice, who, at the writing of this book in 2001, can still belt out sacred songs at the age of 92. "He came in to say hello at the radio station where I worked, WMBI in Chicago. Billy always tells it this way and Cliff and I get a bang out of it: I never had a secretary, but there were several girls in our office who were from a stenographic pool, and Billy tells how he had to go through three secretaries to get to me. What a

line! He dropped in just to say thank you for the programs he was listening to on our station. He was a student at Wheaton at that time.

"Later, he had this radio program, 'Songs in the Night'," Bev said, "and he asked if I would go and be his musical director. He wanted me to conduct a little choir and sing solos, and that's how we got together. I still have the letters from Billy and my replies to them when he

---

Good Visit

The visit to the White House was a highlight of Billy's summer. He thought Mr. Reagan was in excellent physical condition. The president must have tempted him with stories of his horseback riding, for Billy came back wondering how much a good horse would cost.

— Dr. T. W. Wilson, 1981
Associate Evangelist

In Royal Chapel
Elizabeth Hears Graham Preach

WINDSOR, England, May 22 - U.S. evangelist Billy Graham preached to Queen Elizabeth today in a royal chapel. The Duke of Edinburgh, the Queen Mother and Princess Margaret also heard the American minister.

Later Graham and his wife lunched with the Queen.

Graham, obviously affected by the singular honor, told reporters afterwards; "I can only say it was a great privilege to be at Windsor today and that the Queen was very charming and gracious to us."

The sermon to the royal family was a surprise climax to a handsome evangelist's seven-week Scotland-England crusade, which reaped more than 77,000 "Decisions for Christ." The fact that the 36-year-old North

Carolina preacher was invited to conduct a private service for royalty could not help but lift his prestige-already at high tide in Britain.

Queen Elizabeth is titular head of the Church in England and "defender of Faith." Graham is an ordained Southern Baptist minister, be he has always been at pains to emphasize an interdenominational approach in his crusades.

As is the custom with private royal engagements, a spokesman for the royal family would give Windsor today. Graham's associates, usually willing to provide full information about his appearances, had "no comment."

But it was understood from other sources that Graham took for his text Acts 27:25: "Wherefore, sirs, be of

good cheer: For I believe God that it shall be even as it was told me."

Graham, who was making his first appearance in a royal chapel spoke about 25 minutes, a little less time than he ordinarily devotes to sermons at his crusade meetings.

Graham preached in the private chapel at Royal Lodge Windsor near Windsor Castle.

It was Graham's first meeting with Queen Elizabeth, but not his first with persons highly placed in Britain. Last year he called on Sir Winston Churchill, then prime minister, and chatted 40 minutes. During his London crusade last year, Dr. Geoffrey Fisher, arch-bishop of Canterbury and primate of the Church of England, appeared at one of his meetings

The church of England has never officially endorsed Graham's crusades, but has tactily given them strong support.

Graham closed his revival meetings in Britain last night with an impassioned sermon before 90,000 in Wembley Stadium. The British Broadcasting Corporation carried his words and a commentator described how several thousand came forward to make "Decisions for Christ."

Attendances at Graham's meetings in Britain this year totaled 3,139,365.

Graham leaves for Edinburgh tonight to attend a general assembly of the Church in Scotland. Next Sunday he will go to Paris to continue his crusade meetings.

ASHEVILLE CITIZEN-TIMES - MAY 23, 1955

talked about our getting together in Charlotte in 1947. It has been a wonderful association since that time."

Bev has lived in Montreat, N.C., for more than two decades, not far from Billy's mountaintop home, but at the time of this interview, in 1977, he lived in Western Springs, Ill.

"When we got together," Bev said, "Billy said that I must move to Western Springs. I told him I couldn't because I didn't have any

money. I lived in an apartment in Chicago, but the doctors had just told me that Irma should move out of the city for her health.

"A friend in New York City who knew my circumstances heard about this and insisted that I accept the down payment of $2,500 on an $8,900 home. I have added to it several times and still live in it. I got the loan paid back in about eight years.

"Oddly enough," he said, "Billy chose the house. Western Springs was near Wheaton and made it handy for us to work together. Billy asked me to come over and see a house. There were three houses for sale on that street, but Billy had already picked one out. I remember he said, 'This is where you're going to live, Bev,' and I can see him laughing yet. Sure enough, the house Billy chose was the one we liked, so we bought it.

"It has been a great experience, staying with the team and I have enjoyed the work very, very much. I've worked at various times at other projects than the crusades. For eight years, I had a Club Time program for Club Aluminum on ABC. We had to do it live because recording tape wasn't yet in use, and during the Los Angeles crusade in 1949 I had to fly back and forth from L.A. to Chicago to do the show.

"And then I have had the ministry of recordings," Bev said. "For RCA I did forty-eight albums, and I've been with Word now for two years (1977) and have done two with them. That's been a great delight—and it helped put my kids through college."

When Bev mentioned that he had taken voice lessons for seventeen years, Cliff showed surprise. "Gee, I didn't know you'd had any," he said in jest. "I've told people you never had any. I told them that Bev sings so easily he never had to have a lesson. I have never heard Bev vocalize once, warming up—mi, mi, mi,

Billy Graham Calls On Ike, Talks Of Spiritual Matters

WASHINGTON, March 6 - Evangelist Billy Graham called on President Ike Eisenhower today and said he told him a tremendous moral awakening has taken place while Eisenhower has been in office.

Graham said it has been an unparalleled awakening to which he thinks the President has contributed by his church-

going and things he has said.

Graham also said he told Eisenhower that "the moral spiritual quality is our greatest defense as well as our greatest offense." He said the President did not disagree with that.

The evangelist told newsmen his 25-minute talk with the President dealt with mostly spiritual things.

THE REV. BILLY GRAHAM leaving the White House.

ASHEVILLE CITIZEN-TIMES - JANUARY 29, 1956

Opposite: Billy Graham with North Carolina Governor Jim Hunt, 1980.

photo by Ewart Ball

Left: Billy with Russian leader Boris Yeltsin, 1991.

special photo provided by the Billy Graham Evangelistic Association

Below: Billy in a meeting with Russian leader Mikhail Gorbachev, 1981.

special photo provided by the Billy Graham Evangelistic Association

Ethel Waters, Knoxville Crusade, May 1970. photo by June Glenn Jr.

mi! You know, prima donnas come to town and you hear them in a hotel room warming up for two hours before they sing. I never heard Bev open his mouth once."

"Well, I have," Bev said. "A couple of times when I sang at Presidential Prayer Breakfasts, I got up really early and sang into a pillow. Walked around the room singing in a pillow. I just wanted to make sure."

"Bill practices his voice in a pillow," Cliff revealed. "He'll shout, 'Yes! Yes! Yes! Yes!' If Ruth and Bill are riding together in a car, all of a sudden he'll shout, 'Yes! Yes! Yes! Yes!' and Ruth will counter with, 'No! No! No! No!' "

"Billy and Ruth have a lot of fun together," Bev said. "They really do, to be a Baptist and a Presbyterian. I remember a few years ago, I asked Billy, without really meaning it, 'Do you want me to become a Baptist?' I'm a Methodist, but he said it didn't make any difference. He likes variety."

Cliff added, "What denomination we belong to has been the last concern. Five or ten years ago a lot of people asked how we got to be members of the team. Did we have to serve an apprenticeship? The answer is, no, we didn't. It's difficult for them to understand. We never went out and said we need a guy here and we need a guy there. But as a need arose in the development of the ministry God brought across our path somebody uniquely qualified to fill that need, someone we could have good rapport with. I think of Charlie Riggs. What a

Man Walks 400 Miles to Hear Graham Preach at Madras, India

MADRAS, India - Among many thousands of people who poured into Madras from all parts of India to hear Billy Graham was one man who walked over 400 miles. He preached at villages along the way.

When told about the man Billy replied, "I am not worthy of preaching to that man. I should be sitting at his feet."

One hundred people from Hyderabad, 800 miles away, rode a train four days and nights. They had been praying in a 24-hour chain for weeks that God would bless India through Billy.

When all accommodations in town were gone people went from house to house seeking rooms. Hundreds slept in the open. They had come to hear a man who had the peculiar talent for talking about God in a language that people could understand.

Morning meetings at 7 o'clock and evening meetings at 6 o'clock were scheduled for three days. The morning meetings were held for ministers, with more than 5,000 on hand at dawn for the first meeting.

Over 30,000 turned out for the evening rally. Some of the people sat at the site all day. About 3,000 were present by 2 p.m. Billy has had larger crowds but there was something different about this one. People, some dressed in rags and others in the finest silk robes, sat there on grass mats and waited. Most were barefooted. Men and women never sit together in church. There was no hum of conversations. People were quiet. It was an unreal quietness.

There were two choirs of 300 each. One sang in English, the other in Indian dialect. And Indian band played music which had a foot-patting beat to it.

Billy stepped up to the mike. He had two interpreters instead of the usual one. The message had to be translated into Telegu and Tamil dialects. He would stop after each phrase or sentence and had plenty of time to scratch his head before time to speak again. India has hundreds of dialects. People can live 20 miles apart and not be able to understand each other. Billy spoke about a man by the name of Jesus Christ. Some of the people in the strange congregation had never before heard of

Him. To others Christ was just one of thousands of other gods, but Billy described Him as the only God, with Bible quotation "I am the way, the truth and life. No man cometh unto the Father but by Me." He added: "Many Indians seem to have the idea that Christianity is a western religion. That is wrong. There were Christian churches in India before America was discovered. Christ was an easterner. His skin was not as light as mine and it was not as dark as yours." A wire service dispatch quoted Billy as saying Christ was a Negro. He did not say that.

He described Christ as the only road to heaven and then told eager listeners they could only get there by repentance of sin and receiving Jesus by faith.

He gave the invitation. The response was immediate. The front aisle was filled in minutes. Some of those standing before the platform wore a tiny dot in the forehead—the sign of a Hindu holy man. A man knelt with his face in the dust. Pitiful little children with their ribs showing stood looking up. Members of high and low castes stood side by side. The front aisle was becoming dangerously filled and Billy had to ask people to stand where they were. In a counseling room a total of 1,389 signed decision cards. But over 4,000 Gospels of John were given out. There were not enough Tamil, Telegu and English counselors to go around.

On the second night 904 signed cards and over 1,000 signed decision cards the third night.

Probably the most impressive service of the Madras meeting was a morning address to 7,000 students of the area. Billy stressed the folly of rejecting Christ because the human mind cannot understand all about Him intellectually.

Two hundred and fifty students responded to the invitation. A missionary in India for many years said, "These are the finest young men and women in India. This is the first time anyone has ever reached their hearts with the Gospel of Christ." His eyes were filled with tears.

During three days in Madras Billy spoke to over 100,000 Indians and recorded about 4,000 decisions for Christ. Bulganin and Khrushchev didn't do as well.

ASHEVILLE CITIZEN-TIMES - JANUARY 29, 1956

great guy! He was in the oil wells and when he came to be with us in 1952 he was just helping around the office. But God brought him for a purpose. When Bill talks about preparation of materials, like the Bible studies given to those who come forward, he said we have had the finest minds prepare them, and we have: minds like Charlie's. He had walked with God and he knew the Word, and he could communicate it on a layman's level. His importance to our ministry cannot be measured." Riggs directed many crusades.

I asked what had been their toughest crusade, and Cliff and Bev answered simultaneously, "Altoona!"

"That was in '47," Cliff said, "and we haven't been back. There were reasons it was our toughest. One was a woman in the choir with a mental problem. She was a big woman who was given to seizures, and when she made up her mind to do something, it took three ushers to hold her back. Grady (Wilson) had to make a flying tackle on her to keep her from getting to Bill while he preached. The choir was on the platform with all of us, and one night she came out of the choir and went right for Bill at the microphone. Grady tackled her about three steps from him. She was determined and she was strong. One sweep of her hand and everybody would be out of her way."

"Billy didn't know they had a revival meeting every year," Bev said. "To them this was just a yearly performance like their other revivals. The chairman of the crusade, a small fellow, came around and asked Billy to sign a statement that he wouldn't cooperate with a certain group. Billy said he couldn't do that. He told the man that he preached John 3:16 and that he had come to preach to all of the people. That dear old guy was so prejudiced he made it hard on all of us."

"The crusade was in the Masonic Temple," Cliff said, "and at the time Altoona was kind of a dreary, smoky city with coal dust hanging over it."

Bev added, "We were just getting started, and, my soul! We had enough problems." Bev laughed at a thought. "Billy," he said, "had a little roadster and on the final evening he had it loaded and standing by so he could get out of there right after the benediction. Boy, he was ready to go!"

"There have been cities where we have felt Satanic, demoniac oppression in unusual ways," Cliff said. "One was in France at Touloose, and another was in Nuremberg, Germany. Those were times that we realized that only the power of God and the preaching of the Word, would overcome it. We've seen great victory in these situations, but they have never been easy."

The Coming of Muhammad Ali

BY BOB TERRELL

Princes, presidents, and paupers have warmed themselves by Billy Graham's fire. His hospitality has been open to all who were asked to come, but not any have been more welcome than Muhammad Ali, king of the heavyweight fighters.

As he was driven up the winding road, through two security gates, to Billy's mountain-top home, Ali could not stifle a chuckle. He looked at Billy, driving the somewhat less than new Oldsmobile, and remarked, "I thought you'd meet me in a chauffeured limousine, or at least in a Mercedes or Rolls Royce, but here you came in an Oldsmobile, driving it yourself." Obviously impressed, Ali mentioned Billy's driving four times that afternoon.

"That," he said later, "is the sign of a spiritual person. And then we come to his house made of logs. No mansion with crystal chandeliers and gold carpets, just the kind of house a Man of God would live in. I notice things like that. I thought he'd live on a thousand acres, a big farm, but here we are on top of a mountain.

"Mr. Graham is an humble man," Ali said. "The book says Christ will come as a thief in the night. I'm sure God wouldn't come bragging, 'Hey, I'm God.' He's humble, too."

Ali's visit came on a warm autumn day in 1979, and he was impressed with the famous preacher. He and Billy sat on the porch in rocking chairs with a panoramic view of the Black Mountains before them.

For a while, their conversation was simple. "I watch your fights," Billy said, smiling.

"You do?" Muhammad quipped. "If I'd'a knowed Billy Graham was watching me, I'd'a fought better."

"God has been watching you, too," Billy said.

"I knowed that," Ali returned, "but God

Billy Graham and three time world heavyweight boxing champion Muhammad Ali compare fists, September 17, 1979.

special photo provided by the Billy Graham Evangelistic Association

Bob Terrell and

Billy Graham meet

with Muhammad Ali

at Billy's home

September 17, 1979.

special photo provided by the

Billy Graham Evangelistic

Association

and Billy Graham too. . . ." His voice trailed off in feigned awe.

Then they got down to business. With the press present, they chose their words carefully, guarding against saying anything that could be twisted or turned.

"I just wanted to meet him," Ali responded to a question from the press. "From what I can see, Mr. Graham is a real man of God."

Ali commented on the fact that Billy called him mister. "Every time I say Mr. Graham," he laughed, "he says Mr. Ali."

"We have differences," Ali said. "He's Christian and I'm Moslem, but there is so much truth in the messages he gives. He talks about America, repentance, things about government, country, the truth. I've always said if I was a Christian I'd want to be like him.

"He comes before me," Ali said. "I'm a boxer, famous and all that, but he leads people to God. I look up to him."

Ali revealed the reason for his visit. "Basically, I think all religions are good," he said, "and there were a lot of questions I've been wanting to ask about Christianity. So I asked, and he gave me answers.

"I find that titles separate people," Ali said, "Jew and Muslim, Catholic and Protestant, Hindu and Buddhist. But those are man-made titles. Put a Jewish and an Arab heart together on a table and you can't tell them apart. I don't believe God judges man by color or religion, or anything like that. He judges men's hearts."

There were probably several purposes for Ali's visit with Billy, but one seemed to stand above the others. "I've been searching to learn more about other people," Ali said, "The world would be much better if we knew more about each other. I've learned a lot from Mr. Graham today. I wish people who don't like Christians could learn what I've learned. I'd like to see many faiths represented at a conference table to see how they think."

"What I'm trying to do," Ali said seriously, "is figure out what to do. I've had so many offers for major movies and professional contracts. I've turned down three top fight contenders, been offered a network TV show once a month for twelve months interviewing people like Begin and Sadat. I've been asked to manage fighters. But I feel a spiritual pull.

"Muhammad," said Billy, speaking of the man who started the Moslem religion, "went to the cave for forty days to pray and search. He considered Jesus Christ to be a great prophet. In the religion he founded, many things are different from our religion, but many things are the same. The Koran accepts prophets of the Bible like Isaiah, Elijah, and Jesus."

Then he added, "There are other areas we could not agree on, like whether Christ was the son of the Living God. Still, whether we like it

Who Signed the Bible

During Muhammad Ali's 1979 visit with Billy Graham at his Montreat home, Billy autographed a Bible and gave it to the heavyweight champion.

Ali could not decipher Billy's scrawl, which at times resembles chicken tracks. He turned the Bible this way and that, peering at the autograph, then asked Dr. T. W. Wilson, Billy's chief associate, what it said.

T. W. said, "It says 'God Bless You, Muhammad Ali,' and it's signed 'Billy Graham'."

Ali handed the Bible back to Billy and asked, "Would you mind printing your name under that so people will know who signed it for me?"

or not, we've got to live in the same world with a terrible arms race. We have to live together or blow up together. As Christians and Moslems, we not only have to be for peace, we have to work for it."

Later, Billy commented on Ali's visit. "Ruth and I were honored to have Ali and his friends to visit. We had several hours of conversation, and he quoted me several poems. He has a fantastic memory, a brilliant mind.

"There are things that make him different from other major sports figures: He has substance to live. What we see on television, fighting and clowning, are only the tip of the iceberg. I believe God has a great future and purpose for him, and I pray God will show him the path to serve humanity and the Kingdom of God. He has wonderful ability to transmit to the world. There are few in the world who transcend all barriers—race, religion, and such—but he is one of them. That puts tremendous responsibility on him, and I promised to pray for him and help him all I can.

"We come from different faiths," Billy concluded, "but there are many things we have in common."

Chapter Two

PLACES

The Inspiring Story Of Adrian McCaskill: At 79, He Followed Graham To Scotland

GLASGOW, Scotland— Old people can feel young in heart again through the inspiring story of Adrian Alexander McCaskill, 79-year-old pensioner from New Orleans who provided a dramatic moment in the All-Scotland Crusade of Evangelist Billy Graham.

The moment came during the middle of a meeting at beautiful Kelvin Hall, scene of the crusade now under way.

A tall figure, gnarled and somewhat bent with age, the McCaskill had arrived late for the meeting and was looking for a seat down front. Failing to find one in the overflow crowd of 16,000, he went out and found a chair. He placed it near the platform, but an usher whispered he would have to move and was leading him down an aisle when Billy jumped from his seat and cried, in a voice which rang through the hall:

"That man—hold that man. Let him turn and face us."

An electric shock spread through the packed throng. The first thought was that someone was making trouble.

McCaskill, wearing an American Army greatcoat stood with downcast eyes as Billy continued:

"This man comes from New, La. He is nearly 80 years of age and has followed us all over the United States. He lives on a small pension—there are very few of you here who could live on it. He saves his pennies and ministers in New Orleans gave him a few dollars to help out.

"I don't know how he got here. I didn't even know he was here. But he is here—and he has a right to seat anywhere in this auditorium as far as I am concerned."

The old man stood straight and tall and his eyes clouded as he looked at the young preacher, who had interrupted his thoughts on a message to express appreciation for a long journey.

An usher allowed him to place the seat near the front.

After the service he was mobbed by the press and well wishers from both sides of the Atlantic.

"God bless you, sir," said some of the people as they pressed shilling and dollars into his hand. Soon his little nap pocketbook was overflowing.

"My, I have never been so famous in all my life," he beamed.

Next day, as the luncheon guest of the writer and George Beverly Shea, soloist for the Graham team, McCaskill told about his experiences.

He first heard Billy Graham speak about three years ago in San Fransisco. Since that time, he has visited every American campaign conducted by the evangelist, managing it all on a 65 dollar-a-month pension and the little he makes selling religious songs he has written. Some of the meetings he attended were held at Houston, Chattanooga, S. Louis, Portland, Detroit, Syracuse and Dallas.

Last year he dreamed of attending the meetings in London but this was just a little beyond his means and dreams. He continued to save pennies, nickels and dollars in hope that he might come to Scotland.

Then came one of the big decisions of his life. The goal was in sight and it looked as if he could make the trip.

"But I felt very deeply that the Lord wanted me to give $100 to a foreign mission project," he said. "The old devil starting talking to me and said 'don't be a fool; you will never get to Scotland if you give $100 of your savings away.'

"I trusted the Lord and gave it anyway. It wasn't a month before I had the $100 back, and more besides."

The old man cried softly as he recalled the statement of the man who sold him his ticket for the journey: "This trip will be the fitting climax for a well spent life."

He added:

"Before I left New Orleans I prayed and asked God to help me witness along the way and win people to Christ. I won a man in North Carolina."

In New York City he boarded the Italia and on the following Sunday aboard the ship he preached a regular morning service. There were some Germans on board and whenever he had the opportunity he recited John 3:16 to them in German. He has learned the Bible's most famous verse in several languages.

After he had disembarked at Plymouth a little girl stuck her head out a porthole and said:

"Mister, you did a wonderful job of telling us about Jesus at the service."

Again his eyes misted as he said:

"It was worth going all the way around the world to hear a little girl say that."

A Baptist lay preacher and mission worker practically all his life, McCaskill, who has no family, expressed hopes of finding some of his forebears in Scotland before he sails for home on April 18. He will be 80 years old on April 15.

"I want to help Billy as long as I am here," he said. His help consists of prayer and witnessing, two things sought more than any other by the evangelist.

"It has been wonderful getting to visit Scotland and see the people. They have so little compared to Americans. You know, we Americans have never really appreciated our country the way we should."

As he finished his meal and pushed back his chair, McCaskill said:

"I would like to visit Paris before going home."

"You see, I know John 3:16 in French, and that's enough to win people for Christ."

ASHEVILLE CITIZEN-TIMES - APRIL 3, 1955

Scottish Newspapers detail Graham's Scotland Crusade

The Citizen-Times is indebted to a Scotsman, Ernest A. Walsh of 9 Gateside St., for sending a bundle of Scottish newspapers that describe Billy Graham's All-Scotland Crusade.

The bundle, addressed to "the Asheville Press, Asheville, near Crab Tree, North Carolina, U.S.A.," was accompanied by a letter in which Mr. Walsh says that Graham "has stirred up the whole nation!...Anything short of Billy Graham's way would have been useless. Our country is now flooded with new spiritual life."

Mr. Walsh's voluntary testimonial is indicative of how profoundly the Scots have been stirred by the messages delivered by the evangelist from Western North Carolina.

The Scottish newspaper show their awareness of the fact that Graham's great crusade was news of major national interest and concern. In them we learn that the Scots admire Graham's "burning sincerity, his modesty, his breadth of outlook, and his sound conception of evangelism."

The Scots, it appears, have opinions that are in accord with the views of Billy Graham's mountain neighbors.

ASHEVILLE CITIZEN-TIMES - APRIL 3, 1955

Glasgow street scene in front of the building where Billy Graham's Crusade meetings were held during his All-Scotland Crusade in 1955.

Citizen-Times file photo

Billy Graham sings a song with a group of Chinese schoolchildren while on a visit to the Great Wall in 1988.

special photo provided by the Billy Graham Evangelistic Association

Electronics Make A Different Type of Evangelism

The old-time evangelist was able to have twenty-five or thirty sermons that he would preach over and over until he got them down to where they were master-pieces. Because of television, I must find new material to preach new sermons all the time. I suspect that I have more sermons than any evangelist who ever lived. I think Billy Sunday had only one hundred sermons. I was counting mine—they number them in the office—and I'm over the three thousand mark in evangelistic sermons. If I go back and get an old one, say ten or fifteen years old, I can't redo it: I have to redevelop it. It has to be in my soul and heart before I can preach a sermon because I have to experience it. Also because of television, I use notes more extensively as I've gotten older. I want my sermons to have more thought content than they used to have, because I'm speaking to such a wide variety of people from Wall Street in New York to the slums of Los Angeles.

— Billy Graham, 1982

A Thanksgiving To Remember

BY BOB TERRELL

November 24, 1977 was a Thanksgiving day that both Billy and Ruth Graham remember well. They were in the Philippines for a crusade and Ruth arranged with the hotel to provide a Thanksgiving lunch for members of the team.

She informed the chef that the menu should feature roast turkey and sweet potatoes, not realizing that some of her order might be rather foreign to Filipino tastes.

When everyone was seated and lunch was served, the turkey was delicious, but the "sweet potatoes" turned out to be mashed Irish potatoes sweetened with sugar.

It was a nice luncheon with everyone chuckling all the way about their "sweet potatoes."

That evening, however, more than made up for the slight faux pas. Filipino president Ferdinand Marcos and his First Lady, Imelda, honored Billy with his first ever State Dinner in the Malacanan Palace.

"I had been to several state dinners," Billy said, "but never one given in my honor."

This was a gala affair with white-jacketed waiters swarming the hall and singers and dancers holding center stage.

President Marcos toasted Billy thusly: "While this hall has celebrated the passing of kings and prime ministers and presidents, it is honored to celebrate with a man like us, a man of common clay.

"These are dark times all over the world. If there is uncertainty today, perhaps we can answer it. Are these material comforts all that man can expect in this world?

"Unless we have a new set of values, our new society cannot be attained. We need not only physical strength and material resources, but you, Dr. Graham, come at a time when we need prayer. I toast the health and success of Dr. Billy Graham."

Billy was obviously moved. "I have rarely heard a head of state," he said, "make so moving a statement about the state of the world."

Billy Graham stands up to slice the turkey as he and his wife, Ruth, celebrate Thanksgiving in Manilla, 1977.

special photo provided by the Billy Graham Evangelistic Association

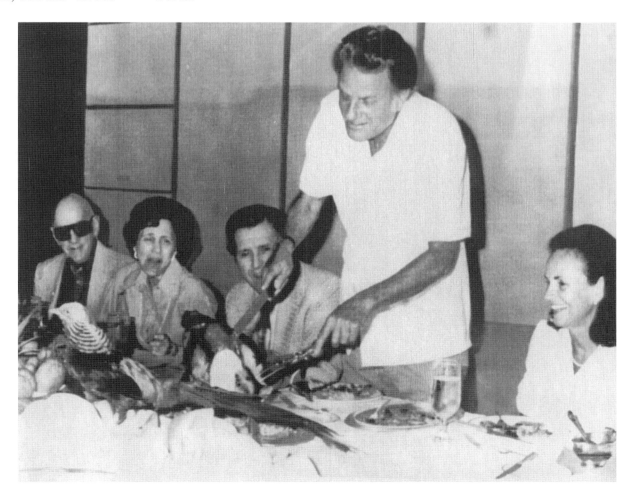

Graham Visits Religious Shrines On His First Trip To Holy Land

JERUSALEM, Jordan Sector (AP)— Billy Graham got a look at biblical scenes and modern problems in the Holy Land Monday. He arrived in the morning for his first visit to the cradle of Christianity.

The American evangelist knelt briefly at the silver star marking the spot where legend says Christ was born in Bethlehem.

He drove to Hebron to see the tombs of the family of Abraham, and visited Gethsemane.

Intermingled with these visits to religious shrines, Graham saw evidence of Arab-Israeli bitterness which has torn the Holy Land apart the last dozen years.

The Jordanian government had blacklisted Graham last November and refused to let him visit the country. He was accused of raising money and propagandizing for Israel in the United States. The ban was lifted on the recommendation of Jordan's ambassador to Washington.

Driving in from the airport, Graham looked across the rubble-strewn no man's land from the Arab side and saw Israel on the other side. On the road from Jerusalem to Bethlehem he could look up the hillside and see Israeli sentries manning gun positions.

Just before reaching Bethlehem he saw vast refugee camps where Arabs who fled from their homes during the 1948 Palestine war have been living in tents or tiny huts ever since.

The strain of his two-month tour through Africa is beginning to show on Graham. But he said he is determined to make the most of his visit to the Holy Land.

He was up at 4:30 a.m. to take the plane to Jerusalem after an exhausting schedule in Cairo. As soon as he landed in Jerusalem he went directly to Hebron and Bethlehem and was still visiting holy places by late afternoon.

"Sure, I'm tired," Graham admitted. "But I don't get to Jerusalem every day."

Even though tired, Graham faces another busy day Tuesday. His schedule has been changed so that he has an audience with King Hussein in Amman on Tuesday instead of Wednesday. At 5 p.m. he preaches in Jerusalem.

Thursday he travels to Nablus to visit an estimated 300 remaining survivors of the Samaritan community.

Graham obviously pleased at his reception from the Christian community in predominantly Moslem Egypt.

Graham estimated at least 2,000 decisions made for Christ in the crowd of 10,000 at Cairo Saturday night.

Looked at on a percentage basis that was just about the largest number of Decisions for Christ we ever had in a single meeting," Graham said.

"We all were amazed at the size of the crowd. and the tremendous interest they showed in Cairo. I never preached to a crowd more filled with anticipation and expectancy."

Noting that Christians in Egypt have lived as a minority for centuries, Graham said, "It's not always easy to be a Christian minority. But the enthusiasm those people showed made me believe there are signs of revival in Egyptian Christendom."

DURING EVANGELIST BILLY GRAHAM'S recent visit to Egypt's pyramids, he received a kiss from a camel.

ASHEVILLE CITIZEN-TIMES - MAY 15, 1960

The Opening of Eastern Europe

BY BOB TERRELL

The Love of God—and of Billy Graham—for the socialistic countries of Eastern Europe, eventually caused changes in the way Man views each other across the globe.

At the start of his evangelistic ministry in the late 1940s, Billy was outspoken against communism, and in 1960 had his first brush with that ideology in Berlin.

A huge tent seating 20,000 was erected near the Brandenburg Gate, the main crossing point between East and West Germany, and Billy planned a seven-night crusade in the tent from September 26 through October 2.

Thanks to the electronic amplification to allow 20,000 people to hear him, Billy's voice carried clearly across the line from West to East Germany.

The communist government immediately closed the gate to East Berliners to prevent their attending the meetings, but thousands crossed at other points and attended anyway.

On the third day of the crusade, East Berlin's acting mayor, Waldemar Schmidt, demanded that the tent be moved "or suffer the consequences," but Billy, with the backing of West Berlin mayor Willy Brandt, defied the edict and continued to preach.

The evangelist told The Associated Press in a telephone interview that he saw no reason in all this to keep him from preaching. "My word!" he exclaimed, "I've been in much more difficult situations than this."

He might have been referring to January through March of that year when he preached many times through Africa, surviving perils and pitfalls along the way.

Too, his defiance of the East German command lay in the fact that it would take a week to move the tent, and that there was no convenient place nearby to re-erect it.

According to the AP, "The Reds stationed dozens of people's police and at least two armored cars close by." West Berlin countered by stationing "bus loads of officers around Billy's tent and escorted him to and from his hotel."

The meetings were concluded without incident on the second of October and the tent was removed.

For many years then, the socialistic governments of Eastern Europe would not allow Billy Graham to come into their lands and preach the Gospel.

In the late 1970s, with the Cold War behind them, something happened in the communist–ruled countries and attitudes began to change. Religious services were and had been held in communist countries, including the Soviet Union, but were almost always state-controlled and monitored.

A learned man came upon the scene then,

Naming a Crusade

Before the 1977 Billy Graham Crusade in his home town of Asheville, N.C., the crusade committee met to put a name to the crusade. One of Billy's associates, Sterling Houston, came from the Minneapolis office to attend the meeting, knowing already, I suspect, what the Graham people wanted to name it, but he wanted the committee to feel that it had had a part in the titling. "We want to work two things into the name of the crusade," Houston said. "We want to get Mr. Graham's name in it and we want to get the mountains in it."

Someone spoke up quickly. "Let's name it the Hillbilly Graham Crusade?"

They quickly settled for the Western North Carolina Billy Graham Crusade.

Billy Graham visits the Brandenburg Gate March 8, 1990, where nearly two miles of the Berlin Wall came down since his last visit six weeks earlier. He stopped to greet several groups of Germans arriving from East Berlin. He also spoke (through his inter-preter) with several East German border guards, giving each of them a copy of the Gospel of Mark and inviting them to the meeting to be held later in the week just a few hundred yards from the Brandenburg Gate.

special photo provided by the Billy Graham Evangelistic Association

Hungarian-born Dr. Alexander Haraszti, a scholarly gentleman then a noted surgeon of Atlanta, Georgia. He began making discreet inquiries in Eastern Europe about the possibility of admitting Billy Graham to preach the Gospel, assuring the governments that there were no hidden desires. Dr. Haraszti made several trips into Eastern Europe, expressing Billy's desires to preach there, usually accompanied by Dr. Walter H. Smyth, vice president of International Ministries for the Billy Graham Evangelistic Association, and Dr. John Akers, a top Graham aide.

Suddenly, in 1977, the way was cleared in Hungary and Billy received an invitation from the Hungarian churches and the government to come and preach. Negotiations behind closed doors succeeded in the issuance of an official invitation for

Billy to visit Hungary in September and an eight-day stay was arranged for September 3-10.

Surprisingly, the Hungarians placed no restrictions on Billy's preaching. "They gave me complete liberty in what I wanted to say," Billy said.

The Rev. Sandor Palotay, president of the Council of Free Churches of Hungary, was host to the Graham team. He was a short, quiet man who went about his business with a calm mien, although he clearly understood what was at stake. This was a trial run, for sure, and all the eyes of Eastern Europe—indeed, of the world—would be focused upon Hungary for those eight days.

After Billy's opening statement of his first sermon, delivered in the beauty of a Hungarian forest high above the Blue Danube, in a camp called the Tahi Youth Camp, things went smoothly for the remainder of the trip. Billy said in that statement: "I do not come here as a politician or official representative of any government," and his words were translated by Dr. Haraszti to 15,000 who had gathered in a clearing in the woods. "I am instead an ambassador of the Kingdom of God. We live in critical times. There are times when it seems that humanity itself is on the verge of chaos and even suicide. We Christians must see our Christian responsibility to do what we can for peace. We must do what we can to help save mankind from tragedy and injustice and nuclear destruction."

He then launched into the same evangelistic sermon that he had been preaching for thirty years, and the crowd was responsive.

After that, Billy preached in Budapest, Debrecen, and Pecs, and was well received by the officials and people of those cities.

Nowhere did Billy step across any line to present anything other than the pure Gospel,

A New Kind of Emotionalism

It is a new kind of emotionalism. Billy does not encourage hosannahs or amens, and he frowns on the shouted response. Too much noise makes him nervous. He is no rookie at his business, but he still gnaws at his nails before he goes on, and he drains himself of energy as he damns the wicked. . . . The people are hungry for something they have not been getting from their leaders, and their emotionalism is heading toward the old-timey right. Mr. Graham is stamping out sin with both feet.

—Author Robert C. Ruark, 1952

and at the end of his Hungarian stay, he commented: "This was the first trip, and they were very nervous as to what I might do, but now I think they have a measure of trust that I'm not going to take advantage of the situation and that I'm going to stick pretty close to the gospel, and that I do recognize that the Church in Hungary has accommodated itself to the state, to live coexistently with the state. None of the clergy are members of the communist party, and there is a separation of church and state with some measure and some guidelines for the church. I think the church is more evangelically minded than a lot of Americans think it is. They certainly seem to love the Gospel."

The socialistic countries responded favorably to Billy's preaching, and the following year, 1978, he preached for eleven days in Poland. And then, in 1982, twenty-two years after he had refused to move his tent in West Berlin, Billy preached for eight days in East Germany, followed by a four-day series of sermons in Czechoslovakia.

In 1984, Billy toured the Soviet Union, preaching in Moscow and Leningrad in Russia, Novosibirsk in Siberia, and Tallinn in the Baltic state of Estonia. A 1985 preaching tour of Romania was attended by hundreds of thousands of Romanians, who relished his every word.

It may have been coincidental, although many observers think not, but soon after these Eastern European campaigns were finished, the great, cold walls of suspicion and hatred between East and West began to crack and crumble, culminating finally with the destruction of the Berlin Wall.

"I think it is true," Dr. Haraszti said, "that Mr. Graham's visits were a prime factor in the lessening of hostilities in that part of the world, which led to better relations between East and West. The government leaders understood that Mr. Graham was in no way a representative of the United States government, but at the same time it was known to them that Mr. Graham was a close companion and perhaps a confidant of presidents of the United States.

"At first, the Eastern governments were suspicious that Billy's motives for coming were not based entirely on religion, and I think that first trip, to Hungary, was something of a test run to see what else

Mr. Graham might have had in mind.

"However, Mr. Graham and his team made such an impression of honesty and genuine concern for the spiritual well-being of the Hungarian people, that the entire Eastern European bloc sat up and took notice."

Whether Billy Graham had anything at all to do directly with the lessening of the political strains between East and West, or whether his appearances in those Eastern European countries were incidental but at the same time a dramatic contribution toward peace, will never be fully known.

But the stress between East and West did begin to slacken soon after that. It is not so strange that many observers credit Billy Graham with such a large hand in the lessening of world strain by applying large doses of the Gospel. Religion was a thing that the communist world had long tried to kill or at least drive underground, but religion appears to have proven the fact that God does, indeed, work in mysterious ways.

Graham Preaches Peace In Hitler's Stadium

NUERNBERG,— Nuernberg, a city which spawned the Nazi party and witnessed many of Hitler's ponderous power orgies in huge Soldiers' Field, turned out 65,000 strong Sunday afternoon to hear an American talk about peace instead of war.

Evangelist Billy Graham spoke from a platform near the spot from which the German fuhrer often watched his troops and tanks pass in review.

Americans will remember shots of the scene as Hitler stood on the top balcony, with a swastika waving at his back, and 500,000 soldiers standing at attention in the arena.

Billy didn't speak from the top platform. By choice, he spoke at the foot of a big cross on a level more even with the people. The marble structure on either side stretched a distance equal three city blocks. The seats were filled with many of the same Germans who had taken part in the other events.

During the Nazi games there were lighted urns of oil at the top of the columns. The urns were without fires for a religious event. A banner underneath each proclaimed "Jesus Christ is the Light of the World."

One German pastor, who had stood on the same field as a storm trooper, said, "The spirit of love was here today. The other time it was a spirit of hate."

Hundreds of American GI's mingled with the gaily dressed Bavarian, some of whom wore the unique leather shorts with shoulder straps.

Shortly before the program was scheduled to begin the clouds darkened, lightning flashed and a few drops of rain fell. It appeared that a deluge would sweep over the packed throngs any minute, but the rain never came.

Something similar happened the

With an interpreter at his side, Billy Graham preached to some 30,000 Germans in Frankfurt on June 21, 1955 to open his tour of Germany.

night before in Neckar Stadium at Stuttgart, where 60,000 gathered to hear Billy. The wind whipped great clouds of dust across the stadium and it appeared that rain would wash out the proceedings. Billy asked the people to pray that God would hold back the rain. The meeting began and the clouds continued to threaten, but the rain didn't come. Even the disinterested observers noted that rain fell in nearby areas on all sides of the stadium but none touched the meeting. Ten minutes after the benediction, the rains came down heavily. "Many people considered this a miracle," Billy commented the next at a press conference.

At the Nuernberg meeting he preached, in the main, the same message he used in addressing 175,000 during the past week, with over 7,000 decisions for Christ "God commands men everywhere to repent and turn to Jesus Christ, the Son of God, by faith,"

he said. "I don't care who you are. I don't care how much money or power you have. I don't care how many times you have gone to church. The Bible says you will never see the Kingdom of Heaven unless you renounce your sins and surrender your will to Jesus Christ."

When he gave the invitation, it was almost impossible for the people to move forward because they were too tightly packed. But they came anyway. The first to step forward was a lady who appeared to be in her 70's. A blonde Aryan youth followed her. Then came sores of others, including GI's in combat boots. A later check disclosed that 2,500 had signed cards indicating their decision and church preference.

Germans and Americans stood together with Billy, at the foot of the cross. And they had love in their hearts for one another.

ASHEVILLE CITIZEN-TIMES - JUNE 30, 1955

All The Talk About God As Chiangs Entertained Billy

TAIPEI, Formosa—"We have tried everything the devil had to offer and found they don't hold water."

The metaphors may be a little mixed up, but the woman doing the talking didn't seem to be. She was Madame Chiang Kai-shek, one of the world's most talented and beautiful women.

The setting was ideal for polite chit-chat, but the chit-chat turned into a theological discussion. Sitting across the table from Madame Chiang at the presidential palace was her husband, the Generalissimo, once ruler of the biggest nation on earth. He lost some of his world popularity when he committed the "great sin" of being opposed to communism, U.S. Ambassador Karl L. Rankin was at one end of the table and his wife at the other. On each side of Madame Chiang was Billy Graham and Cliff Barrows, his music director. A few other guests were present, including Dr. Frank Graham, founder of Christian College in Formosa, and Dr. Robert Pierce, head of World Vision.

Chinese food was being served and for a few minutes there was a hum of conversation among the guests. Then Madame Chiang began asking questions. Most of her questions were directed at Billy Graham. The hum faded as everyone strained to hear the conversation between two of the world's most famous people.

One of the first things she asked was "Are people save who make a decision for Christ and then backslide?" Billy answered, "If the decision was genuine I believe the Bible teaches they are saved, but if a person has sincerely received Christ into his heart he isn't going to stay a backslider long. He will be so miserable that

MADAME CHIANG
. . . **growing in Christian experience**

he will ask God's forgiveness and resume living like a Christian. Some people who think confessing Christ gives them a license to sin are just kidding themselves. They have never been saved."

Madame Chiang has stated she was an intellectual Christian. For many years she believed in God with her head but not her heart. It was only in recent years, she said, that she experienced Christ in a real way and began to grow.

The Generalissimo took little part in the conversation. He doesn't speak English. His face brightened occasionally when Dr. Frank Graham, a gifted linguist, or his wife would

interpret a choice bit. Only an outstanding diplomat could have sat there looking pleasant while listening to words he couldn't understand.

The next question Madame Chiang asked was this: "What about people who have never heard of Christ? When they die will they go to hell?"

One person at the table replied immediately: "They are lost." Madame Chiang countered, "I don't believe that." Billy said:

"I don't believe any man can set himself up a judge and say whatever these people are lost or saved. I think that rests in the providence of Almighty God, a God who is holy, pure and righteous. I do believe that the Spirit of God deals directly with some people who have never heard His message. Jungle savages have been found worshiping Christ who have never seen a Bible or listened to a preacher."

One couldn't help but marvel at the nature of the conversation around the dinner table of Nationalist China's Number One family. All of the talk was about God, the Bible and Jesus Christ.

After the guests left the table and retired to the drawing room Generalissimo answered a few questions through an interpreter. A faithful reader of the Bible, he said his favorite verse was the 23rd Psalm. He said that it was his dream to lead his people back to the mainland of China.

In reply to the question as to what would be his Number One prayer request to the Christians of the world, he said he would ask that people would be willing not only to pray about stopping communism but to do something about it when they have finished praying.

• • •

ASHEVILLE CITIZEN-TIMES - JUNE 30, 1955

Opposite: People couldn't get into the crowded church during Billy Graham's visit to Moscow in 1982, so he spoke to them outside. *photo by Bob Terrell*

Left: Kindergarten class in the Soviet Union, 1982. *photo by Bob Terrell*

Below: Locals made a festival out of the 1977 Billy Graham Crusade in Manila.

photo by Bob Terrell

Into The Valley Of The Shadow

BY BOB TERRELL

Into the Valley of the Shadow we rode, first by chartered plane from Madras to Vijayawada, and then by Indian Air Force helicopter to the devastated area of southeastern India. Not one of us was prepared for what we saw. A tidal wave, generated by a cyclone in the Bay of Bengal, struck late the afternoon of November 19, 1977, driving an 18-foot wall of water into the Indian countryside, inundating an area 50 miles long and 15 miles deep. Three million people were rendered homeless. At least a hundred thousand lost their lives, India president Neelam Sanjiva Reddy had told Billy Graham in Delhi two days earlier.

There were five of us from Billy's team, Dr. Walter Smyth, who directed Billy's international affairs; Photographer Russ Busby; a television team, Frank Johnson and John Lenning; and me. It was my job to keep the news services abreast of Billy's visit. Because of Billy's stature in the world, we were the first non-governmental people to be taken into the devastated area, and the very first, we were told, to set foot in the worst stricken area.

Our Russian-built helicopter thundered

over hundreds of square miles where no moving traffic, no sign of humanity could be seen. We landed at three villages—Avanigadda, an inland farming village, and Sorlagondi and Gollapalem, fishing villages on the coast of the Bay of Bengal. Not any of us will forget what we saw.

Billy came away from those places with tears flowing down his cheeks. "This," he said, "is one of the great disasters of the twentieth century. It is far worse than the world has been told." The press services had previously reported 9,000 dead in the tidal wave.

In Avanigadda, huge fields of sugar cane and vast paddies of rice, only a week away from harvest, lay ruined in the slime, the land so saturated with saline that it would be two years before farmers could try another crop. In Sorlagondi, where the tidal wave struck first, only three of 400 homes remained standing. Nine hundred of the village's 2,000 population had been violently killed. Clothing remained entangled in the wicked thorn bushes standing throughout the remains of the village—a sari here, a shirt there—ripped off victims as the wall of water hurled them through

Opposite: South-eastern India from a helicopter, 1977 photo *by Bob Terrell*

Above: Tidal wave devastation in Southeastern India, 1977. photo by Bob Terrell

Sorlagandi, India in 1977. Girl dead 20 days after the tidal wave. photo by Bob Terrell

gotten down in the mud with her lowest caste, the poorest people on earth, who owned little more than the loincloths they wore, and he was moved. That evening he telephoned his headquarters in Minneapolis and asked how much money they had in the Emergency World Relief Fund. He was told $238,000, and that evening he wrote a check for that amount, which he gave next day to church-related organizations that would put every cent to work among the suffering people.

He also pledged to the Rt. Rev. Sundar Clarke, bishop of the Church of South India, which encompasses protestant denominations, that the Billy Graham Evangelistic Association would rebuild every church destroyed in the tidal wave, regardless of denomination. More than 100 churches, mostly thatch-roofed structures, were destroyed in the flood. Two years later, the villages in which churches had been rebuilt had come back to life. Those that had no churches had not.

the brush. While Billy toured Sorlagondi, prisoners from local jails, pressed into the service of burying and burning the dead, discovered the blackened corpse of a young woman, 20 days dead, and while Billy prayed and the villagers stood with heads bowed, her body was burned on a bier of dried saw grass and lodge poles.

In Gollapalem 2,000 of the village's 3,000 residents died in that terrible rush of water, villagers pushed forward to kneel before Billy as he stepped from the helicopter into the thick mud. Few of them knew what Christianity was, but they had been told that Billy Graham was a "holy man," and they clutched at his knees, deeply moved that a holy one would come to share their grief in this land of hundreds of religions.

An old man clutched Billy's knees and wailed in Telugu, "Help us rebuild our homes, or kill us!" Tears fell from Billy's cheeks into the mud at his feet. He was told that the old man had lost eight family members in the disaster.

"I was in Korea and Vietnam at the height of war, and in Guatemala last year after earthquakes devastated that country," Billy said, "but never have I seen destruction as total as this." Earlier in that three-weeks trip, Billy had seen India's glitter and gold, but on this day he had

His Greatest Work

Most Americans think of Billy Graham as an electronic evangelist whose piercing eyes, stabbing finger, and urgent voice exhort sinners into the Kingdom of God, and, indeed, that is his calling, his life's work. He is widely seen on television, going about his Father's business in gigantic, worldwide crusades, but the full extent of his ministry does not show through. His concerns are global, and the arms of his ministry reach into the palaces of kings and the halls of Parliament, but they also extend to the loneliest shepherd in the field, with whom he does his greatest work.
— Bob Terrell
Asheville (N.C.) Citizen

Caretaker of the governor's snakes, in Madras, India, shows off a King Cobra to Billy Graham and other guests. This caretaker had been bitten 20 times by cobras at the time this photo was taken in 1977.

special photo provided by the Billy Graham Evangelistic Association

Opposite: Billy on horse-back at Hortobagy Farm in Hungary, 1977.

special photo provided by the Billy Graham Evangelistic Association

Left: Billy attempts to "saddle up" out on the Hungarian plain, 1977.

special photo provided by the Billy Graham Evangelistic Association

Below: Billy and crew on their way to the Hortobagy Farm, Budapest, Hungary.

special photo provided by the Billy Graham Evangelistic Association

Opposite: Ruth poses in a window in the Fisherman's Bastiom on the Buda side of Budapest. The city is divided into Buda and Pest by the Danube River.

special photo provided by the Billy Graham Evangelistic Association

Left: News conference in Budapest, 1977. From left to right, Billy, Dr. Alexander Haraszti (liaison representative for Eastern Europe), Dr. Sandor Palotay (president of the Free Churches in Hungary), and Dr. Walter Smythe (director of Graham's overseas operations.

special photo provided by the Billy Graham Evangelistic Association

Below: Billy talks with people outside the Sun Street Baptist Church in Budapest after the revival meeting, 1977. These people were unable to get into the church so Billy went out to see them.

special photo provided by the Billy Graham Evangelistic Association

Opposite: Cliff Barrows, Billy Graham and Alexander Haraszti eating goulash in Hungary, 1977.

special photo provided by the Billy Graham Evangelistic Association

Below: Billy offers a gift to Pope John Paul II. This hand-carved shepherd scene (left) was made by Bob Terrell from native North Carolina trees.

special photo provided by the Billy Graham Evangelistic Association

Chapter Three

THE SPORTSMAN

Opposite: Billy on the golf course in 1955.

photo by June Glenn Jr., Citizen-Times

Left: Billy meets the first coach of the Atlanta Falcons, Norb Hecker, who trained at Blue Ridge Assembly near Black Mountain, 1966.

Citizen-Times file photo

Billy's Love for Sports

BY BOB TERRELL

Just as his predecessor Billy Sunday did, through his growing-up years Billy Graham dreamed of playing major league baseball and was often found on the sandlots of Charlotte playing the game he loved.

Billy Sunday's dream came true. That noted evangelist played eight seasons in the major leagues with Chicago, Pittsburgh, and Philadelphia, all in the National League. His baseball roots were so deeply set that after he left baseball and began evangelizing, he would run on stage and slide into the lectern.

Billy Graham's dream failed to materialize. He began preaching when in his teens, but his love of sports never diminished. In addition to baseball, he played golf, bowled, probably took a few licks at a tennis ball, and at least on one occasion went bear hunting.

He was often in attendance at baseball games of the Asheville Tourists professional team in Asheville's McCormick Field, especially in the early years of his ministry. He attended the games until his prominence in

Opposite: Billy hunts with professional bear hunter, Bill Gibbs from Lake Tahoma, in the Black Mountains.

photo by Bob Terrell

Left: Billy goes for a strike at an Asheville bowling lane in the early 50s.

photo by June Glenn Jr.

he evangelical world grew so large that he could no longer watch the games because of people wishing to talk with him.

The bear hunt was prompted by the gift of a beautifully engraved shotgun by an Indian rajah. No bears were seen on that day, and it is doubtful that Billy would have fired at one if he had seen it.

Billy loves the wholesomeness and cleanliness of organized sports and often follows sporting events like the Olympics and the World Series on television. He realized the value of sports to the physical fitness of the nation, a point that had emphasis in each presidential reign during Billy's career.

He first played golf cross-handed, making it all but impossible for him to make a straight shot, and after he switched to a more conventional grip, his game improved.

His favorite golf course was that in his home town, the Black Mountain Golf Course, and even though he wasn't a par-shooter, he adorned his game with occasional excellent shots.

Among his acquaintances were and are many of the world's great athletes. When the Atlanta Falcons trained near Black Mountain to open their first professional football season, Billy visited a time or two and had his picture made with several of the burly football players.

He was friendly with several golfers and other athletes, but perhaps the one who made the greatest impression on him was Muhammad Ali, the heavyweight boxing champion of the world, whose spiritual faith lay deeper within him than his boxing skills.

Opposite: Billy swings his way out of a sand trap at Biltmore Forest Country Club, November 5, 1971.

photo by Bert Shipman

Right: Inner tubing down the Boise River in 1982.

special photo provided by the Billy Graham Evangelistic Association

Below: Billy meets Falcon players Bud Erickson, Errol Linden in 1966.

Citizen-Times file photo

Opposite: Billy gets some golf advice from Billy Joe Patton, top amateur at the Masters in 1954.

photo by Bob Terrell

Graham Likes Rain

CHARLOTTE, N.C.—Rain which threatened the opening of Billy Graham's Charlotte crusade didn't worry the evangelist. Asked if the rain would cut attendance, Graham, who later had an overflow audience of 14,375, replied: "No, I think it might help. At least, it will drive the golfers in."

ASHEVILLE CITIZEN-TIMES
SEPTEMBER 22, 1958

Chapter Four

THE MAN

Left: Billy Graham preaching in

Washington, 1952.

Citizen-Times file photo

Happiness

You don't find happiness by going after it, but by doing your duty and your relationship with your fellow man and with God.

—Billy Graham

> "I might not have gone into full time evangelism if it hadn't been for Ruth. I listened to her in 1949 when she told me that evangelism was my calling after the Hearst newspaper chain began publicizing me."
>
> —Billy Graham

A Helping Hand

One Sunday morning shortly after my husband's death, Ruth Graham called and offered to leave a pot roast in my oven for Sunday dinner. When I returned from church I found that Ruth had not only left the pot roast but had also cleaned my oven.

—Ann McCay
Graham neighbor

Opposite: Billy and Ruth Graham in the early 50s.

Citizen-Times file photo

Below: Billy Graham and his family, reunited at their home Montreat following his Australian Crusade and European tour, July 1959. From left to right, Gigi, Bunny, Ruth, Franklin (in back), Ned, Billy and June. photo by June Glenn Jr.

A Matter Of Mortality

Evangelist Billy Graham says he thinks he will see Elvis Presley in heaven and is "pretty sure" he will die within the next ten years. "I never met Elvis, but I believe I will see him in heaven because Elvis Presley was very deeply religious, especially in the last two or three years," Graham said. . . . Graham said he foresees his own death in the next ten years because of his family's history. "My father had his first stroke at my age now (59). Well, I have the same problems he had — I've got high blood pressure and these other symptoms, so I look forward to it. I mean death to me offers no fear at all — it only has anticipation. I'd be glad to get away from the pressure under which I live every day and get in the presence of Christ, and I hope He lets me rest a while and then gives me another job somewhere else, because I really believe that I am going to a literal heaven."

—The Associated Press, 1977

Perturbed Truck Driver Aided By A Real Expert

On a Sunday morning this month a truck driver paced the floor of a service station on Tunnel Road, east of Asheville. He had troubles—the kind of troubles that eat a man's heart out.

The owner of the station listened sympathetically, as he had been doing at intervals all week. He wanted to help the fellow—console him—but he didn't know how.

The cars thickened around the gas pumps. The owner of the station went outside to help. A late model car drove up and parked. The man under the wheel was alone—nice looking, neatly dressed. A second look showed he was an old customer who hadn't been in for several weeks.

They come from all walks of life, mused the proprietor as he wiped the windshield, but this was indeed a study of contrasts. He wondered how it would be to bring the two men together.

"A friend of mine inside the station is in pretty bad shape," he said. "I can't help him but maybe you can. Have you got time to come in and talk with him?"

"Sure, I have time," the man answered, with a smile.

After introducing the men, the proprietor left them talking in a corner of the service station. He did not want to eavesdrop, but he couldn't help hearing parts of the conversation as he journeyed back and forth between the cash register and the gas pumps outside.

Some 15 minutes later the two men left. The service station operator felt a warm glow inside as he recalled fragments of the conversation he had overheard:

"I can't help you-and really I don't know whose fault it is—but God can help you—I'm on my way to church. Won't you come with me? It doesn't matter if you're not dressed—we'll sit in the back row in the balcony—no one except God and He won't be looking at your clothes. Of course, I'll wait for you, if you want to dress—I promise. Come on, let's go...

The telephone rang. The proprietor answered.

"Have you seen him? I'm worried sick—simply worried sick..." asked the voice on the other end of the line.

The proprietor paused a moment, then answered, "Yes—he was here a little while ago but he's gone to church now with Billy Graham."

ASHEVILLE CITIZEN-TIMES - NOVEMBER 30, 1958

Basics Are The Same

The basics of a Billy Graham Crusade are still the basics of the old-fashioned revival meeting. Sophisticated, I suppose, by modern electronics. Sophisticated too, I hope, by a growth in knowledge from those old days. I listen to old tapes of myself preaching and don't even know it's me. I roamed all over the platform, and I suppose that was the youthful zeal with which I preached.

—Billy Graham

He Needed Another Physical Exam

I've been jammed, pushed, pulled, shoved, and elbowed many times. I've experienced tough crowds at the World's Fair in New York, near stampedes at the World Series, countless jams at college football games, but one of the worst jams I've ever been in occurred at the Asheville Civic Center on opening night of the Western North Carolina Billy Graham Crusade.

John Corbett led, or tried to lead, our church group of 40 persons. We joined thousands of other persons an hour before the start of the crusade, and it was each person for himself, all pushing to get in the building first. Under ordinary circumstances I might have given up and gone elsewhere, but this was a Billy Graham Crusade. Too, no one could have gotten out if he'd wanted to. I doubt if a person had fainted he would have been able to collapse to the floor. It was that crowded.

Once we got in, we had good seats near the back on the main floor, but by then I felt I needed another physical examination.

—Jim Story, editor
Marshall (N.C.) News-Record

A FASHION PLATE?

Along with Billy's bright and interesting
persona came a taste for some
bright and interesting
outfits over the years.

PROLIFIC PREACHER

Billy Graham has preached to more than 82,194,995 people during his career. The following is a list of some of the places he held crusades and the years in which they were held.

Aarhus, Denmark — 1955
Aberdeen, Scotland — 1991
Accra, Ghana — 1960
Addis Ababa, Ethiopia — 1960
Adelaide, Australia — 1959
Albany, New York — 1990
Albuquerque, New Mexico — 1952, 1975
Altoona, Pennsylvania — 1949
Amherst, Massachusetts — 1982
(University of Massachusetts)
Amsterdam, The Netherlands — 1954
Anaheim, California —1969, 1985
Anchorage, Alaska — 1984
Arad, Romania — 1985
Asheville, North Carolina — 1953, 1977
Atlanta, Georgia — 1950, 1973, 1994
Auburn, Alabama — 1965
(Auburn University)
Auckland, New Zealand — 1959, 1969
Augusta, Georgia — 1948

Baltimore, Maryland — 1949, 1981
Bangor, Maine — 1964
Basel, Switzerland — 1960
Baton Rouge, Louisiana — 1970
Beijing, People's Republic of China — 1988, 1994
Belfast, Ireland — 1961
Berlin (GDR) — 1982
Berlin, West Germany —1954, 1960, 1966, 1990
Bern, Switzerland — 1960
Billings, Montana — 1987
Birmingham, Alabama — 1964, 1972
Birmingham, England — 1984
Blackpool, England — 1982
Boca Raton, Florida — 1961, 1981
Boise, Idaho — 1982
Boston, Massachusetts — 1950, 1964, 1982
Boston, Massachusetts — 1982
(Northeastern University)
Bradenton-Sarasota, Florida — 1961
Bratislava, Czechoslovakia — 1982
Brisbane, Australia — 1959, 1968
Bristol, England — 1984

Brno, Czechoslovakia — 1982
Brussels, Belgium — 1975
Bucharest, Romania — 1985
Budapest, Hungary — 1985, 1989
Buenos Aires, Argentina — 1962, 1991
Buffalo, New York — 1988
Bulawayo, South Rhodesia — 1960
Burlington, Vermont — 1982

Cairo, Egypt — 1960
Calgary, Alberta, Canada — 1981
Cambridge, England — 1980
Cambridge, Massachusetts — 1982
(Harvard University - JFK School of Government Memorial Chapel)
(Massachusetts Institute of Technology)
Canberra, Launceston
and Hobart, Australia — 1959
Cape Canaveral, Florida — 1961
Caribbean Tour — 1958
Chapel Hill, North Carolina — 1982
Charlotte, North Carolina — 1947, 1958, 1972, 1996
Chattanooga, Tennessee — 1953
Cheyenne, Wyoming — 1987
Chicago, Illinois — 1962, 1971
Christ Church, New Zealand — 1959
Cincinnati, Ohio — 1977
Clearwater, Florida — 1961
Cleveland, Ohio — 1972, 1994
Cluj-Napoca, Romania —1985
Columbia, South Carolina — 1950, 1987
Columbus, Ohio — 1964, 1993
Copenhagen, Denmark — 1954,1965

Dallas, Texas — 1953
Dallas-Fort Worth, Texas — 1971
Denver, Colorado — 1965, 1987
Detroit, Michigan — 1953, 1976
Dortmund, West Germany — 1955, 1970
Dothan, Alabama — 1965
Douai, France — 1963
Dresden (Saxony) (GDR) — 1982
Dunedin, New Zealand — 1969
Durban, South Africa — 1973
Dusseldorf, West Germany —1954

East Rutherford, New Jersey — 1991
Edinburgh, Scotland — 1991
Edmonton, Alberta, Canada — 1980
El Paso, Texas — 1962
Enugu, Nigeria — 1960
Essen, West Germany — 1960
Essen, Germany — 1993

Fargo, North Dakota — 1987
Fort Lauderdale, Florida — 1961, 1985
Fort Worth, Texas — 1951
Frankfurt, West Germany — 1954, 1955
Fresno, California — 1958, 1962
Fukuoka, Japan — 1980

Gainesville, Florida — 1961
Geneva, Switzerland — 1955
Glasgow, Scotland — 1955, 1961, 1991
Good News Festivals in India — 1977
Gorlitz (GDR) — 1982
Gothenburg, Sweden — 1955, 1977
Grand Rapids, Michigan — 1947
Great Britain — 1967, 1989
Greensboro, North Carolina — 1951
Greenville, South Carolina — 1966
Guangzhou, People's Republic of China — 1988

Halifax, Nova Scotia, Canada — 1979
Hamburg, West Germany — 1960
Hamilton, Ontario, Canada — 1988
Hanover, New Hampshire — 1982
(Dartmouth College)
Hartford, Connecticut — 1982, 1985
Helsinki, Finland — 1954, 1987
Hilo, Hawaii — 1965
Hollywood, California — 1951
Hong Kong — 1975, 1990
Honolulu, Oahu, Hawaii — 1965
Houston, Texas — 1952, 1965, 1981
Hyaiyin, People's Republic of China —1988

Ibadan, Nigeria — 1960
Indianapolis, Indiana — 1959, 1980, 1999
Ipswich, England — 1984

Jackson, Mississippi — 1952, 1975
Jacksonville, Florida — 1961, 2000
Jacksonville, North Carolina — 1962
Jerusalem, Jordan — 1960
Johannesburg, South Africa — 1973
Jos, Nigeria — 1960

Kaduna, Nigeria — 1960
Kahului, Maui, Hawaii — 1965
Kansas City, Missouri — 1967, 1978
Kiev, Ukraine, U.S.S.R. — 1988
Kisumu, Kenya — 1960
Kitwe, North Rhodesia — 1960

Knoxville, Tennessee — 1970
Kohima, Nagaland, India — 1972
Kumasi, Ghana — 1960

Lagos, Nigeria — 1960
Las Vegas, Nevada — 1978, 1980
Lausanne, Switzerland — 1960
Leningrad, Russia, U.S.S.R. — 1984
Lexington, Kentucky — 1971
Lihue, Kauai, Hawaii — 1965
Little Rock, Arkansas — 1959, 1989
Liverpool, England — 1984
London, England — 1954, 1955, 1966, 1989
Los Angeles, California — 1949, 1958, 1963
Los Angeles, California — 1974
(25th Anniversary Celebration)
Louisville, Kentucky — 1956, 1964
Lubbock, Texas — 1975
Lyon, France — 1963

Manchester, England — 1961
Manchester, New Hampshire — 1964, 1982
Manila, Philippines — 1977
Mannheim, West Germany — 1955
Melbourne, Australia — 1959, 1969
Memphis, Tennessee — 1951, 1978
Mexico City, Mexico — 1981
Miami, Florida — 1949, 1961
Milwaukee, Wisconsin — 1979
Minneapolis, Minnesota — 1950, 1961
Minneapolis-St. Paul, Minnesota — 1973,1996
Modesto, California — 1948
Monrovia, Liberia — 1960
Montauban, France — 1963
Montgomery, Alabama — 1965
Montreal, Quebec, Canada — 1990
Moscow, Russia, U.S.S.R. — 1982, 1984, 1988
Moscow, Russia — 1992
Moshi, Tanganyika — 1960
Mulhouse, France — 1963

Nairobi, Kenya — 1960, 1976
Nancy, France — 1963
Nanjing, People's Republic of China — 1988
Nashville, Tennessee — 1954, 1979, 2000
Nassau, Bahamas — 1982
New Haven, Connecticut — 1982
(Yale University)
New Orleans, Louisiana — 1954
New Orleans, Louisiana — 1982
(Southern Baptist Convention Evangelistic Rally)
New York City, NY — 1957, 1969, 1970, 1991
New York City, NY — 1960
(Spanish)
Newton, Massachusetts — 1982
(Boston College)
Norfolk-Hampton, Virginia — 1974
Norwich, England — 1984
Novosibirsk, Siberia, U.S.S.R. — 1984
Nurnberg, West Germany — 1955, 1963

Oakland, California - 1971, 1997
Okinawa, Japan — 1980
Oklahoma City, Oklahoma — 1956, 1983
Omaha, Nebraska — 1964
Oradea, Romania — 1985
Orlando, Florida — 1961, 1983
Osaka, Japan — 1980
Oslo, Norway — 1955, 1978
Ottawa, Ontario, Canada — 1998
Oxford, England — 1980

Paris, France — 1954, 1955, 1963, 1986
Peace River, Florida — 1961
(Sunrise Service)
Pecs, Hungary — 1985
Perth, Australia — 1959
Philadelphia, Pennsylvania — 1961, 1992
Phoenix, Arizona — 1964, 1974
Pittsburgh, Pennsylvania — 1952, 1968, 1993
Poland - 1978
Ponce, Puerto Rico — 1967
Portland, Maine — 1964, 1982
Portland, Oregon — 1950,1968, 1992
Prague, Czechoslovakia — 1982
Providence, Rhode Island — 1964, 1982
Pyongyang, Korea (North) — 1992, 1994

Raleigh, North Carolina — 1951, 1962, 1973
Redstone Arsenal, Alabama — 1962
Relay Services — 1959
Relays - Manchester, England — 1961
Reno, Nevada — 1980
Richmond, Virginia — 1956
Rio de Janeiro, Brazil — 1960, 1974
Rochester, New York — 1988
Rotterdam, The Netherlands — 1955

Sacramento, California — 1958, 1983, 1995
Salisbury, Rhodesia — 1960
San Antonio, Texas — 1958, 1968, 1997
San Diego, California — 1958, 1964, 1976
San Francisco, California - 1958, 1997
San Jose, California - 1981, 1997
San Juan, Puerto Rico — 1967, 1995
Santa Barbara, California — 1958
Sao Paulo, Brazil — 1979
Satellite Locations in Iceland — 1978
Satellite Locations in Norway — 1978
Satellite Locations in Sweden — 1978
Seattle, Wash. —1951, 1962, 1965, 1976, 1991
Seoul, Korea (South) — 1973, 1984
Shanghai, People's Republic of China — 1988
Sheffield, England — 1985
Shreveport, Louisiana — 1951
Sibiu, Romania — 1985
Singapore — 1978
Sioux Falls, South Dakota — 1987
South Bend, Indiana — 1977

South Hamilton, Massachusetts - 1982
(Gordon-Conwell Seminary)
Spokane, Washington — 1982
Springfield, Massachusetts — 1982
St. Louis, Missouri — 1953, 1973, 1999
St. Petersburg, Florida — 1961
Stendal (GDR) — 1982
Stralsund (GDR) — 1982
Stockholm, Sweden — 1954, 1978
Stuttgart, West Germany — 1955, 1963
Suceava, Romania — 1985
Sunderland, England — 1984
Sydney, Australia — 1959, 1968, 1979
Syracuse, New York — 1953, 1989

Tacoma, Washington — 1983, 1991
Taipei, Taiwan — 1975
Tallahassee, Florida — 1961, 1986
Tallinn, Estonia, U.S.S.R. — 1984
Tampa, Florida — 1961, 1979, 1998
Timisoara, Romania — 1985
Tokyo, Japan — 1967, 1980, 1994
Toronto, Ontario, Canada — 1955, 1967, 1978, 1995
Toulouse, France — 1963
Tour-American Cities — 1952
Tour Europe — 1954
Tour-Florida Cities — 1953
Tour-India and Far East — 1956
Tour-New England States — 1950
Tour-Scotland Cities — 1955
Tour-South America — 1962
Tour-Southern States - 1951
Tour-West Coast — 1954
Tour-West Texas — 1953
Turin, Italy — 1967
Tuscaloosa, Alabama — 1965
(University of Alabama)
Tuskegee Institute, Alabama — 1965

U.S. Service Bases — 1955
Uniondale, New York — 1990
Usumbura, Ruanda-Urundi — 1960

Vancouver, British Columbia, Canada — 1965, 1984
Vero Beach, Florida — 1961
Villahermosa, Mexico — 1981

Washington, D. C. — 1952, 1960, 1986
Wellington, New Zealand — 1959
West Palm Beach, Florida — 1961
Wheaton, Illinois — 1959, 1980
Williamsburg, Virginia — 1976
Winnipeg, Manitoba, Canada — 1967
Wittenberg (GDR) — 1982

Zagorsk, Russia, U.S.S.R. — 1988
Zagreb, Yugoslavia — 1967
Zurich, Switzerland — 1955, 1960

$\mathcal{I}$ AM PLEASED THAT. . .

1. Bob Evans founded thirty organizations in Europe because of our crusades.
2. Bill Bright founded Campus Crusades for Christ on our work.
3. I have learned people can serve the Lord in other systems.
4. I've grown more tolerant with people who hold diverse views from me.
5. I still believe in the infallibility of the Bible, the Virgin Birth, the Bodily Resurrection, Blood Atonement on the Cross, and the Second Coming.
6. We Christians have a responsibility toward the poor, the oppressed, the downtrodden, summed up in terms of social justice. More than 1,000 texts in the Bible relate to our service to the poor.
7. My basic message is the same today as when I began.
8. With Youth for Christ in 1945-47 I preached in every state.
9. In 1950 in the Atlanta Crusade I announced I was going to stop love offerings. I decided to form a board, have our books audited, and pay myself a salary only.

$\mathcal{R}$EGRETS

Yes, looking in retrospect, I have some regrets. I would have handled some things differently.

1. I would have put more emphasis on private study and have fewer speaking engagements.
2. I regret I didn't get further training in the seminary.
3. I should have worked more closely with churches. I believe in the Church in all denominations.
4. Unconsciously, being a strong patriotic American, I almost identified the Kingdom of God with Americanism and thought it should be imposed on the world.
5. I should not have made statements construed as political. I was young and uninhibited and hadn't traveled the world.

—Billy Graham